PHOTOGRAPH
SCOTLA

COLIN BAXTER

Colin Baxter

SCOTLAND

Scotland lays claim to being the best small country in the world. It certainly packs a tremendous amount into its 30,000 square miles. Mountains and moors are everywhere, but nowhere more spectacularly than in the Scottish Highlands where the mighty Grampians, the greatest mountain system in the British Isles, reaches from Ben Lomond, just beyond the outer fringes of Glasgow, to Ben Hope in the far north. Deep waters vie with the dizzy heights for attention in the landscape, including 30,000 freshwater lochs and 6,600 rivers; not for nothing is Scotland also known as 'the land of the mountain and the flood'.

Nature's awesome forces created the landscape over millions of years, but men and women have moulded it to its present appearance. In the shadows of the mountains, and beside those rivers and lochs, the landscape is littered with a legacy of human endeavour from our ancient past – mysterious stone circles and monumental tombs from the Stone Age,

mighty hillforts and imposing broch towers from the Bronze and Iron Ages, Imperial Rome's most northerly frontier, the Antonine Wall, and imposing castles and abbeys from the Middle Ages.

The agricultural and industrial revolutions of recent times not only revolutionised the lives of Scots, but transformed the landscape too. The patchwork-quilt cornfields that fringe the 6,000 miles of coastline, and carpet the soft contours of the Central Lowlands and Southern Uplands, owe their origin to the agrarian reformers of 300 years ago. To the industrialists who made Scotland the 'workshop of Empire' in the 19th century we owe the thousands of miles of road, canal and railway that criss-cross the landscape, and our cities and towns. Today, most Scots live and work in the Central Belt, centred on Glasgow and Edinburgh. And yet those high mountains and deep lochs still prevail – just as powerfully impressive as when our remote ancestors first set eyes on them.

THE FIVE SISTERS OF KINTAIL, Loch Duich (left) and CASTLE STALKER, Argyll (above).

LOCH SHIEL (above) and the nearby GLENFINNAN VIADUCT (right), Highland.

TRÀIGH AN T-SUIDE, IONA, & THE ROSS OF MULL, Argyll.

HIGHLAND COW (left) – the mainstay of the Highland crofters' economy for centuries.

EDINBURGH CASTLE AND CITY CENTRE (above) and the Georgian NEW TOWN (right).
Dominated by Edinburgh Castle, Scotland's capital city was founded almost
1,000 years ago, and recently designated a World Heritage Site.

LUSKENTYRE, Harris, Western Isles (right) – the Atlantic coastline of the Outer Hebrides is famed for its wonderful cream-white beaches and turquoise waters. The machair that lines many of the shores of the Western Isles are a haven for wildflowers in Spring and Summer.

THE CALANAIS STONES, Lewis, Western Isles (left) – the ancient circle at the heart of a vibrant Stone-Age community may have been an astronomical observatory 5,000 years ago.

THE RIVER GARRY AT KILLIECRANKIE, Perthshire (left) – where, on 27 July 1689, Viscount 'Bonnie' Dundee defeated the army of William and Mary, and almost succeeded in restoring the Stuart dynasty to the throne of Great Britain and Ireland.

GLEN AFFRIC & LOCH AFFRIC, Highland (right) – one of Scotland's most beautiful glens, hidden away in the mountains between the Great Glen and the Atlantic coast. Beyond are the snow-capped peaks of Kintail way to the west.

BUACHAILLE ETIVE MÒR, Glencoe (left) and OBAN HARBOUR, Argyll (above).

THE EILDON HILLS & RIVER TWEED (above), and the SCOTTISH BORDERS (right).

TORRIDON, Wester Ross, (right)
– the Torridon mountains are the
oldest mountains in the British
Isles. The area, which encompasses
the dramatic peaks of Beinn Eighe,
Beinn Alligin and Liathach was
designated Britain's first National
Nature Reserve in 1951.

PLOCKTON, Wester Ross, (left)
was a planned village created in
the late 18th / early 19th century
that grew into a thriving fishing
centre. Today its picturesque
setting beside Loch Carron has
become a popular tourist
destination in the Highlands.

CAPE WRATH FROM FARAID HEAD, Sutherland, (left) – the often stormy north-western tip of the British mainland is a remote area of broad sandy beaches and rugged cliffs.

BEN LOYAL AND THE KYLE OF TONGUE, Sutherland, (right) – a distant world inhabited by mountains with strange-sounding names, such as Sgòr Chaonasaid, Càrn an Tionail and An Caisteal, at 2506 ft (764 m), the highest of the snow-capped peaks.

LOCH LINNHE, Lochaber, Highland – with the mountains of Kingairloch beyond.

LOCH ETIVE, Lorn, Argyll (left) – with Ben Cruachan, 3693 ft (1126 m) looming up behind.

BALMORAL CASTLE, Aberdeenshire (above) – the Highland home of Queen Victoria and Prince Albert. The creation of their 'dear paradise' in the shadow of LOCHNAGAR (right) and beside the River Dee resulted in the area becoming known as 'Royal Deeside'.

URQUHART CASTLE, Loch Ness (above) – a mighty fortress that has stood sentinel in the 'Great Glen' since Pictish times in the 6th century. LOCH NESS (left), seen from the north end, is by far the largest of the three inland lochs forming much of the Great Glen.

THE NATIONAL WALLACE MONUMENT, Stirling (above) towers above Abbey Craig, the rocky perch from where, in September 1297, William Wallace directed his great victory over the English, the battle of Stirling Bridge. Wallace recaptured mighty STIRLING CASTLE (right) shortly after.

THE FORTH BRIDGE, a Victorian wonder of railway engineering, spans the Firth of Forth near Edinburgh.

PITTENWEEM, Fife (left) – a timeless fishing village in the 'East Neuk' of Fife.

THE ISLANDS OF RUM AND EIGG, Inner Hebrides – looking west from between Arisaig and Mallaig.

GLEN BARRISDALE, Wester Ross (right) – looking towards Loch Hourn and the mountains of Knoydart.

ULLAPOOL, Loch Broom, Wester Ross (left) and LOCH ASSYNT, Sutherland (above).

LOCH ACHRAY (above) and LOCH ARD (right), Loch Lomond and the Trossachs National Park.

CROVIE, Aberdeenshire – a typical fishing village with houses gable-end on to the beach.

CASTLE FRASER, Aberdeenshire (left) – one of the finest late-medieval castles in Scotland.

LOCH BRACADALE, Isle of Skye – looking out across the Little Minch towards South Uist.

THE CUILLIN HILLS, Isle of Skye (right) – viewed from Elgol across Loch Scavaig.

RED DEER (right) – a common sight in the Scottish Highlands. The stags cast their antlers in the Spring and regrow them again for the rutting (mating) season in the Autumn.

BALEPHUIL BAY, Tiree, Hebrides (left) – the tranquility of the island's white strands and fertile machair is disturbed only by the chirrup of the skylark and corncrake, and the ceaseless wind, of course.

CAISTEAL BHARRAICH, Sutherland, (left) – the ancient residence of the Bishops of Caithness overlooks the Kyle of Tongue. Rising in the distance is the mighty Ben Hope 3041 ft (927 m), Scotland's most northerly Munro – mountains over 3000 ft (914 m).

OLDSHOREMORE, Sutherland, (right) – the gnarled knuckles of rock around the bay are Lewisian gneiss, at 2800 million years Britain's oldest rock. The twin peaks of Foinaven and Arkle in the distance, of Torridonian sandstone, were formed just under 1000 million years ago.

THE SKYE BRIDGE & LOCH ALSH, West Highlands – the road bridge was officially opened in 1995.

EILEAN DONAN CASTLE, Loch Duich (left) – a former stronghold of the Mackenzies and MacRaes.

THE ROSS OF MULL & ARDMEANACH, Isle of Mull, Argyll – viewed from the holy island of Iona.

THE VILLAGE, ST KILDA, Western Isles (right) – finally abandoned in 1930 after centuries of existence.

THE STONES OF STENNESS, Orkney – a Stone-Age ceremonial centre from 5,000 years ago.

GAADA STACK, Foula, Shetland (left) – once part of the island's coast, but long since marooned in the sea.

THE CAIRNGORM MOUNTAINS from the north and from above LOCH AN EILEIN, Rothiemurchus (right).
The Cairngorms National Park was established in 2003. It is home to 25% of all of Britain's threatened
birds, animals, and plants – and contains a large area of sub-Arctic mountain landscape at its centre.

BEN MORE, Isle of Mull, Argyll (right) – the name Mull comes from the Gaelic *meall*, 'lump'. The highest point on the island, Ben More at 3169 ft (966 m) is the only island mountain, outside Skye, to be classed as a Munro.

BLAIR CASTLE, Perthshire (left) – the ancestral home of the Murray family, who have held the title of the Dukes of Atholl for centuries. Said to date from 1269, the castle's stunning turrets and embattled parapets are largely Victorian.

THE RIVER SPEY, Strathspey, (left) – writing snake-like down the heather-clad Spey Valley from its source high in the Monadhliath Mountains. The marshes around Loch Insh (top left) are among the most important wetlands in Europe.

LOCH MALLACHIE at dusk, Strathspey, (right) – the remnant ancient Caledonian pines provide ideal nests for goldeneyes, which can be seen diving for food on the placid waters of the loch, here within the Cairngorms National Park.

BRAEMAR HIGHLAND GATHERING, Royal Deeside – attended each year by members of the royal family.

Published in Great Britain in 2007 by Colin Baxter Photography Ltd,
Grantown-on-Spey, Moray PH26 3NA, Scotland
www.colinbaxter.co.uk

Photographs © Colin Baxter 2007
Text by Chris Tabraham
Copyright © Colin Baxter Photography Ltd 2007
All rights reserved.

A CIP Catalogue record for this book is available
from the British Library.

ISBN 978-1-84107-361-3   Printed in China

Page one photograph: THE CUILLIN HILLS & LOCH DÙGHAILL, Skye
Page two photograph: LOCH LOMOND FROM THE AIR
Front cover photograph: BLAIR CASTLE, Perthshire
Back cover photograph: LOCH NA KEAL, Isle of Mull